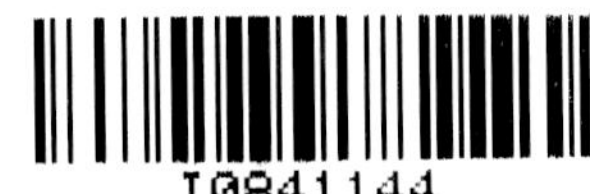

MENAGERIE

A HAND-DRAWN COLORING BOOK BY

SHERRY HARTMAN

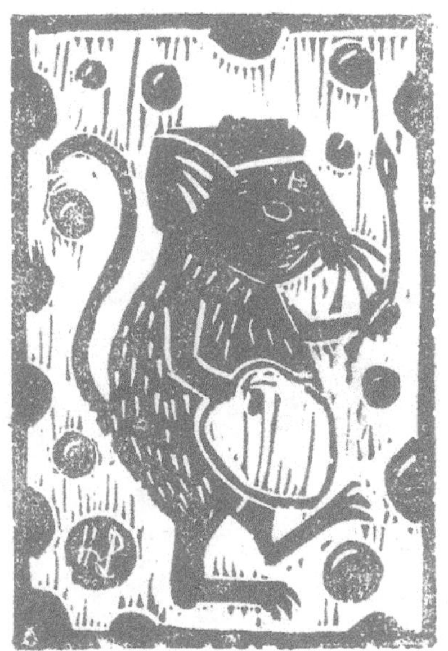

Copyright 2018

Colored by_______________________________

Date_____________________

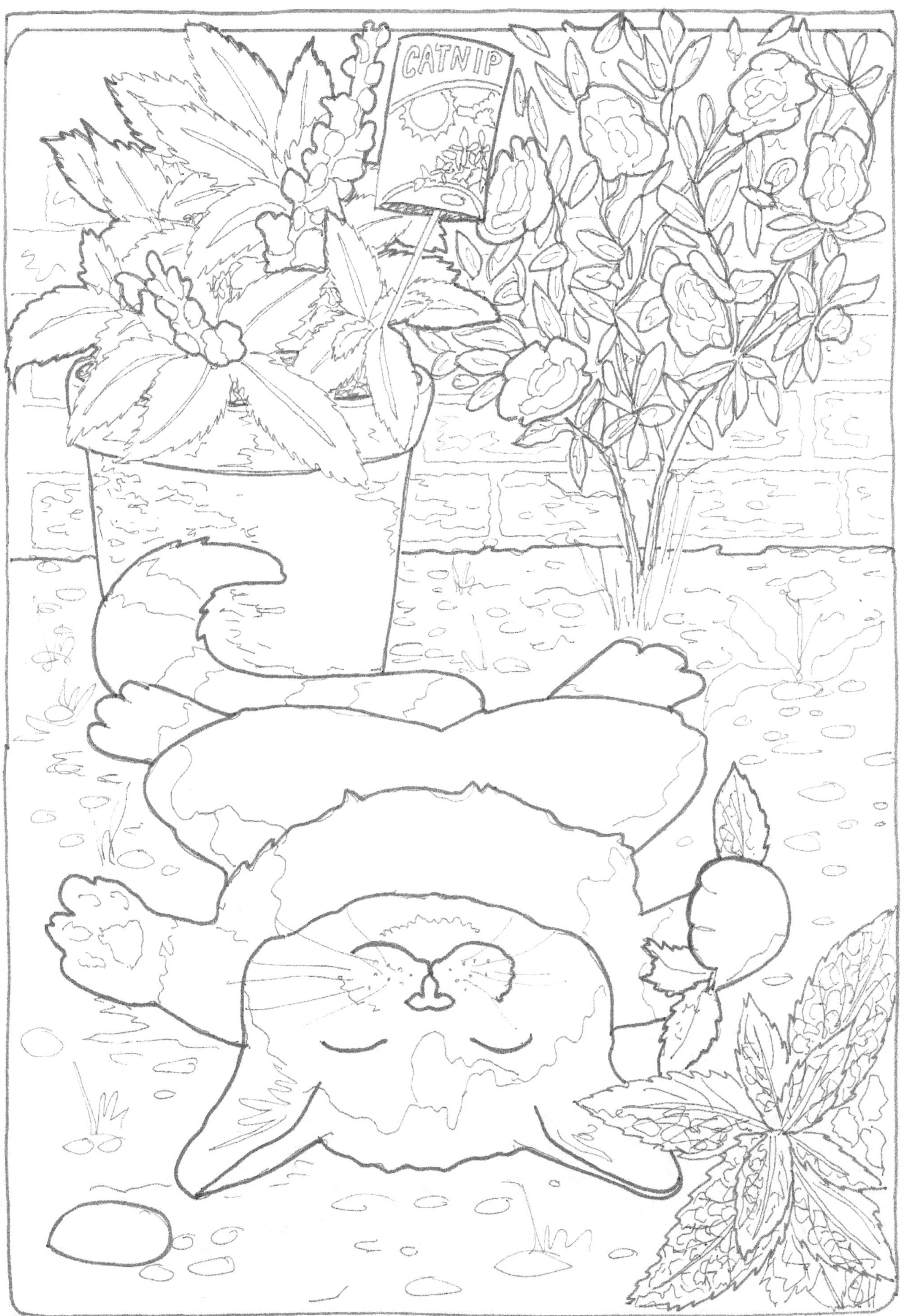
CATNIP

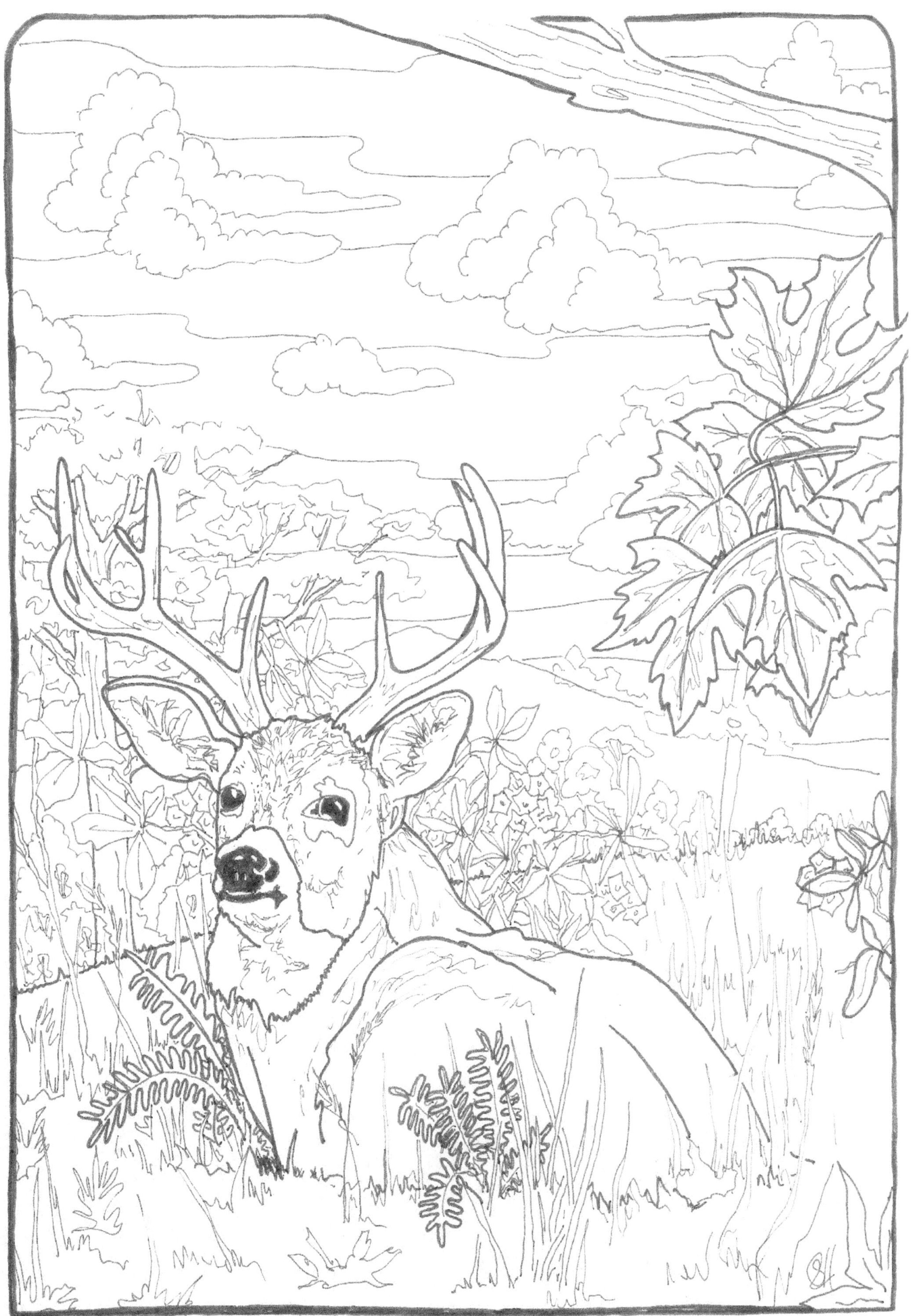

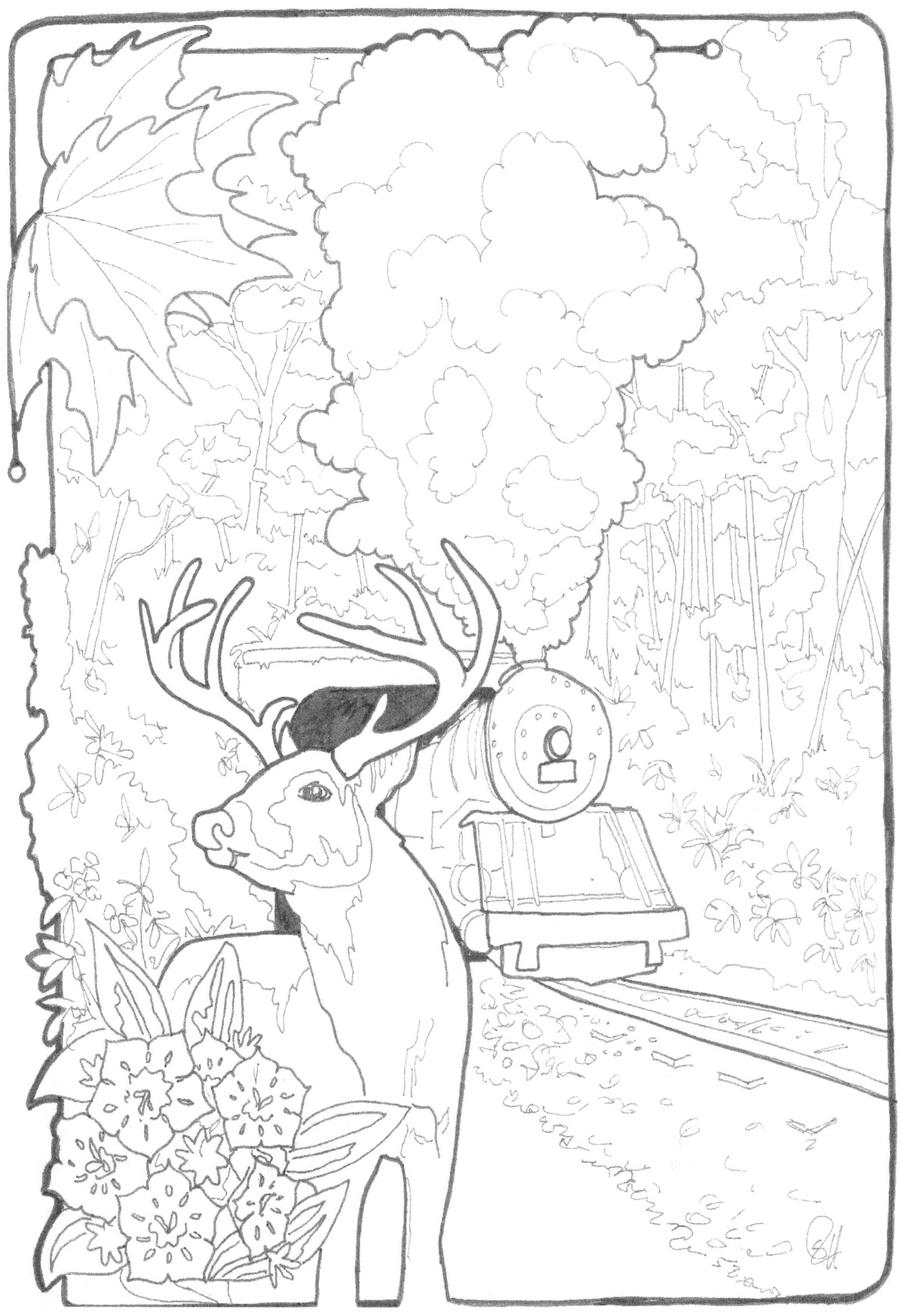

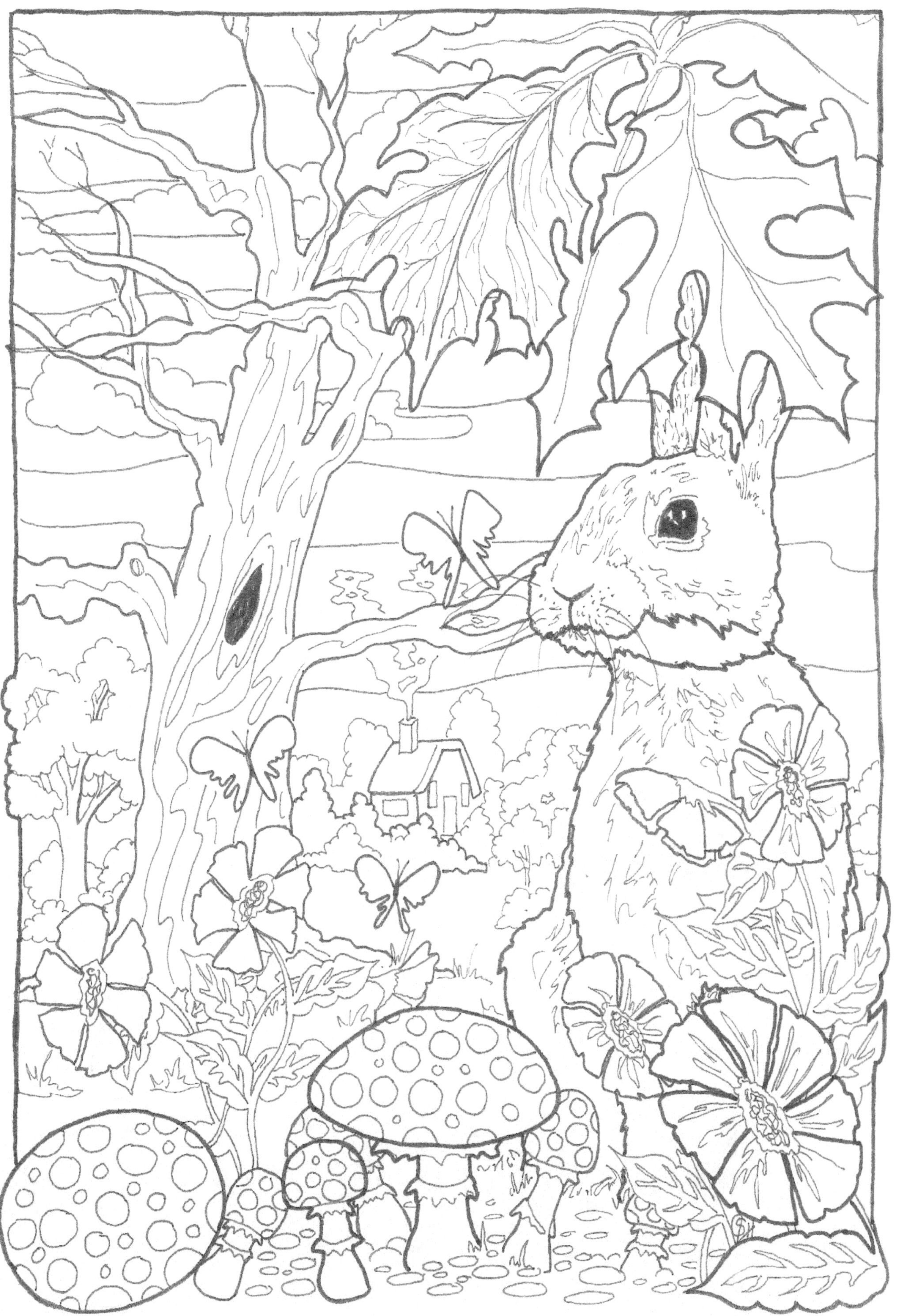

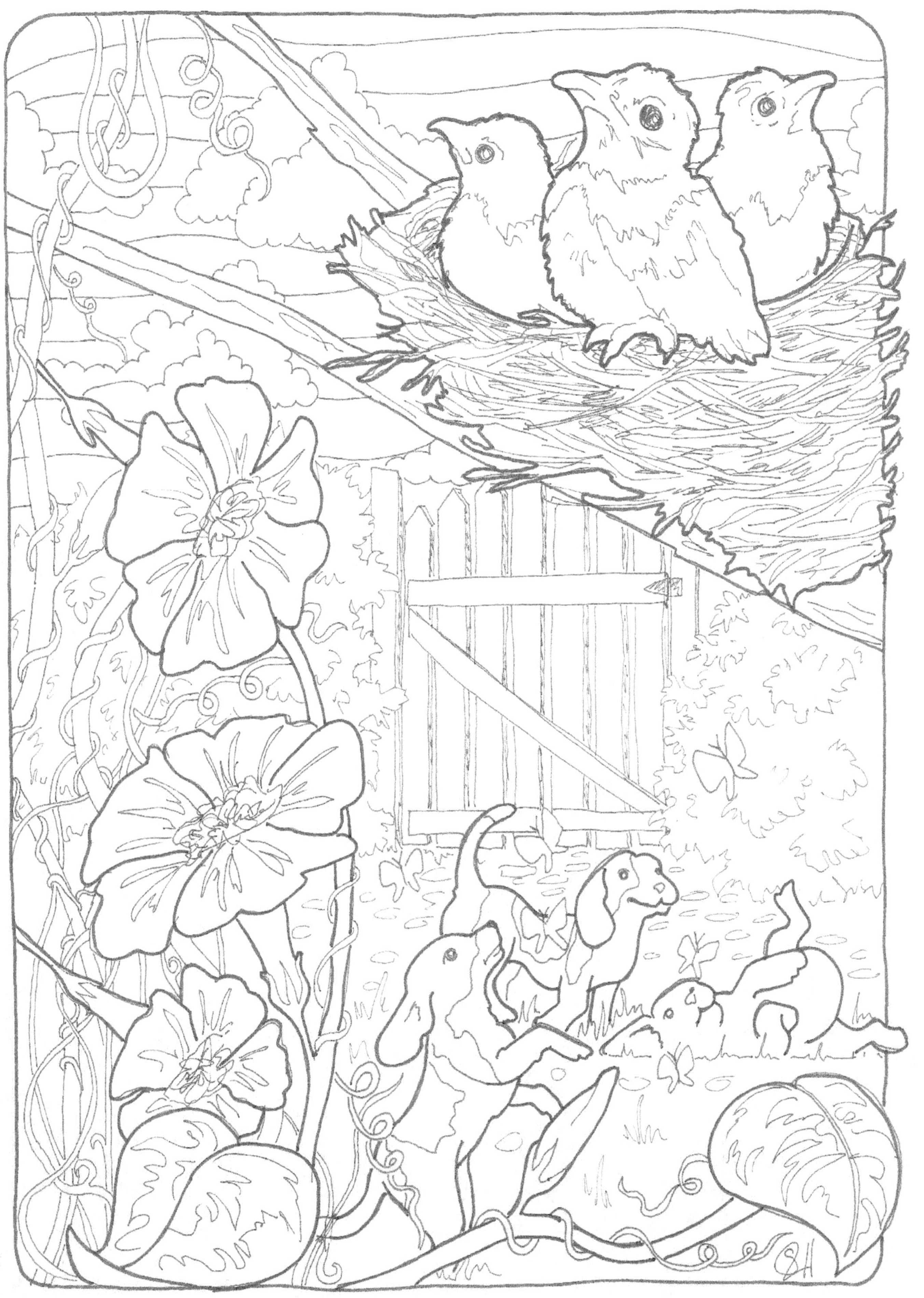

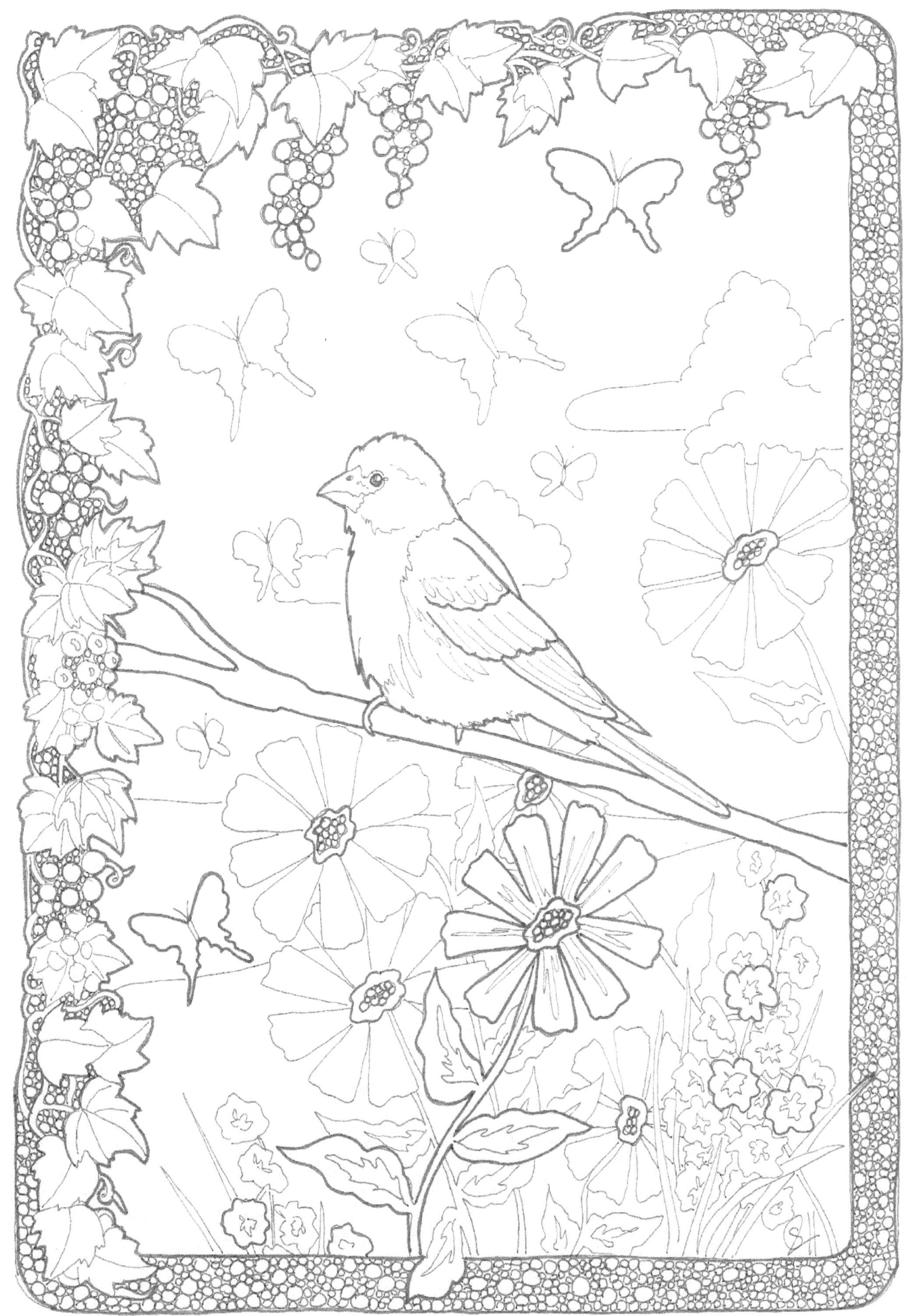

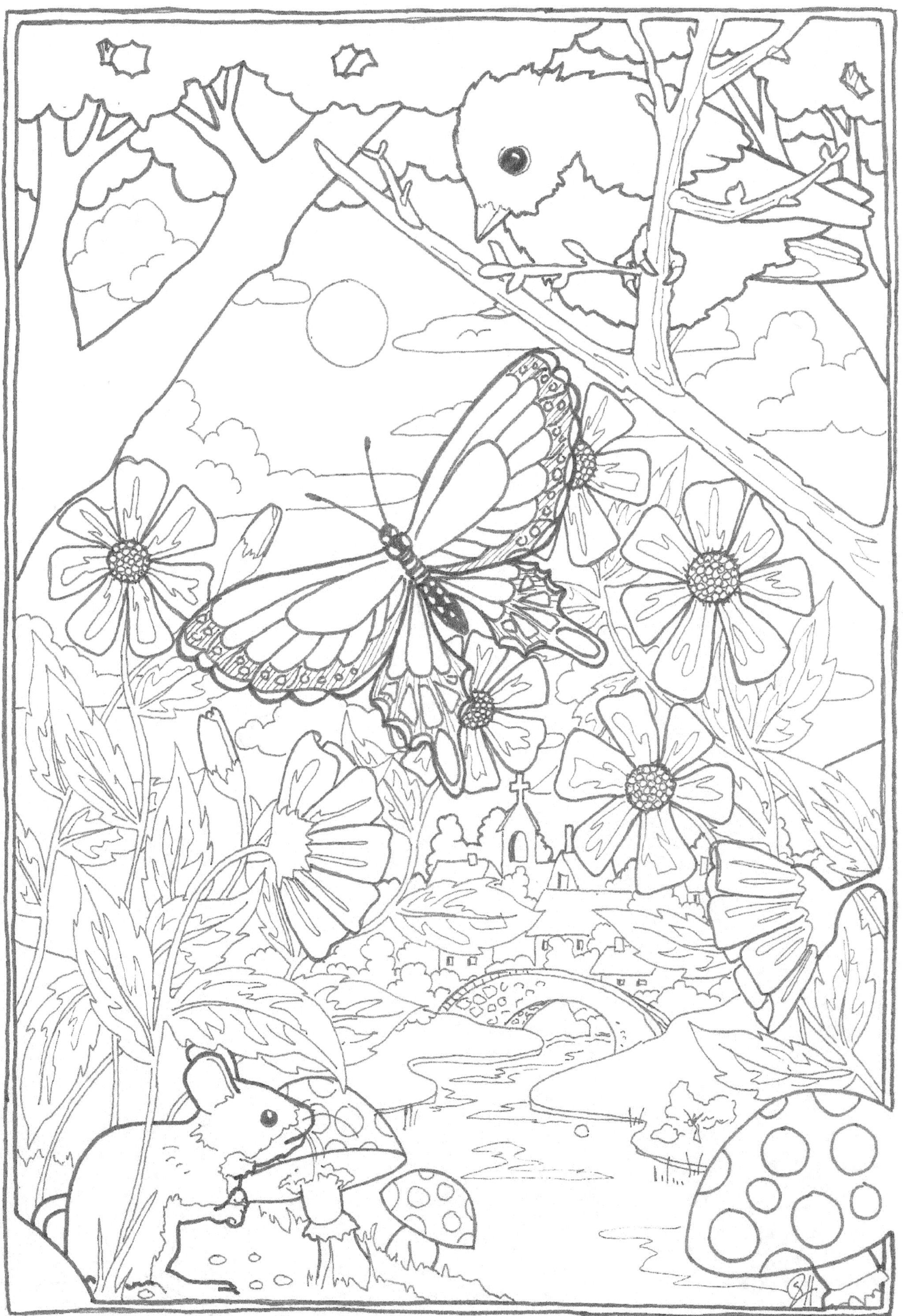

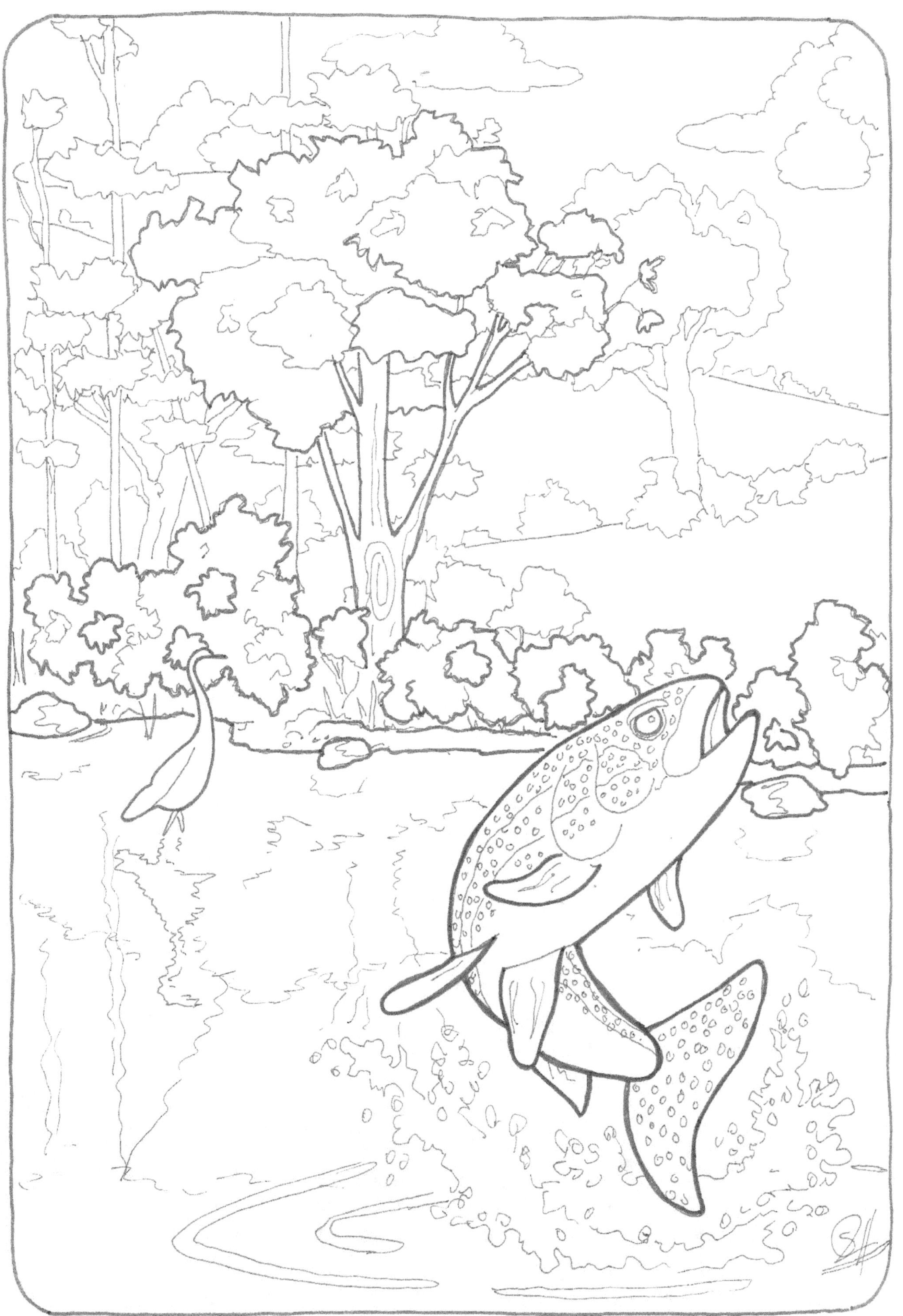

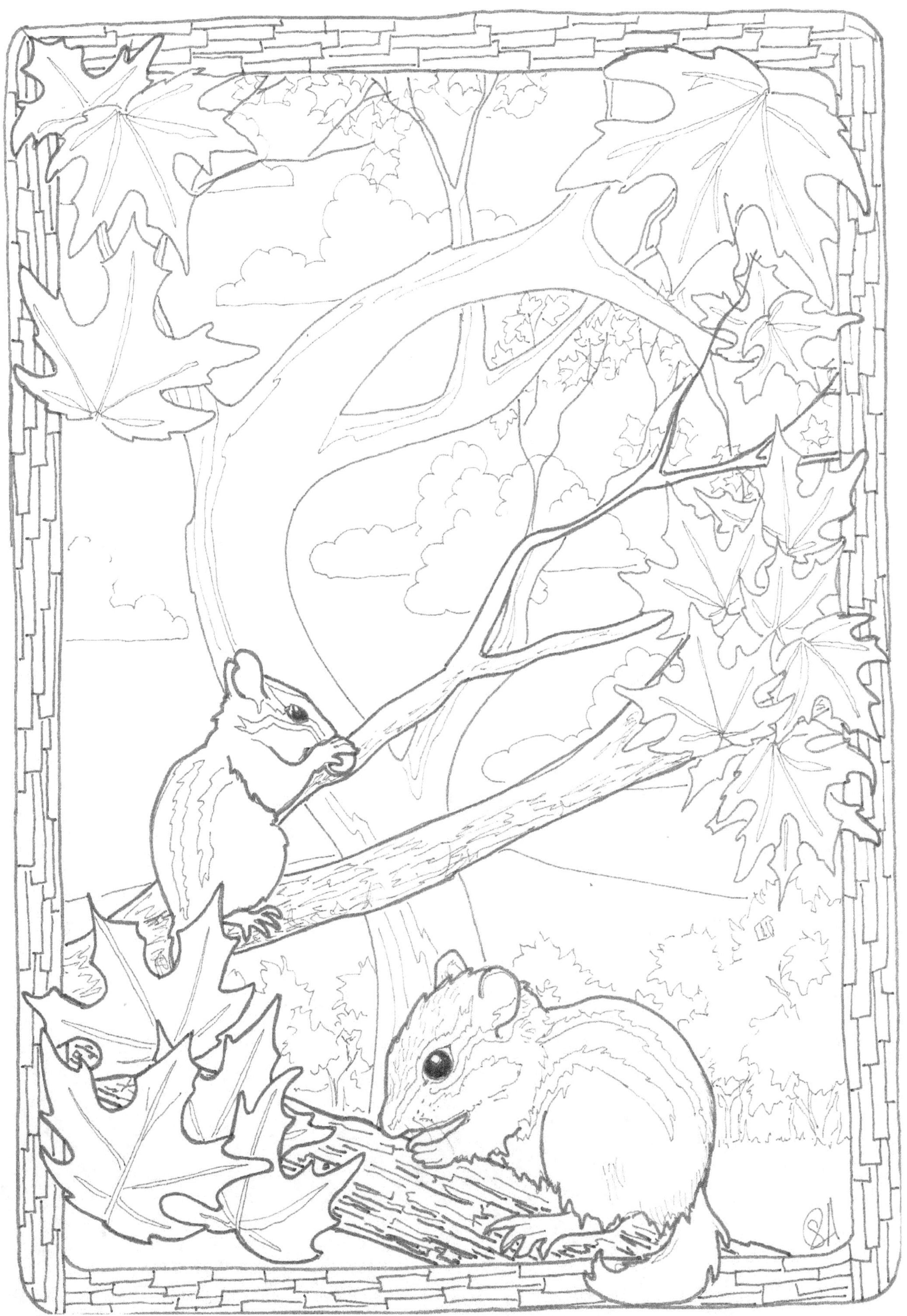

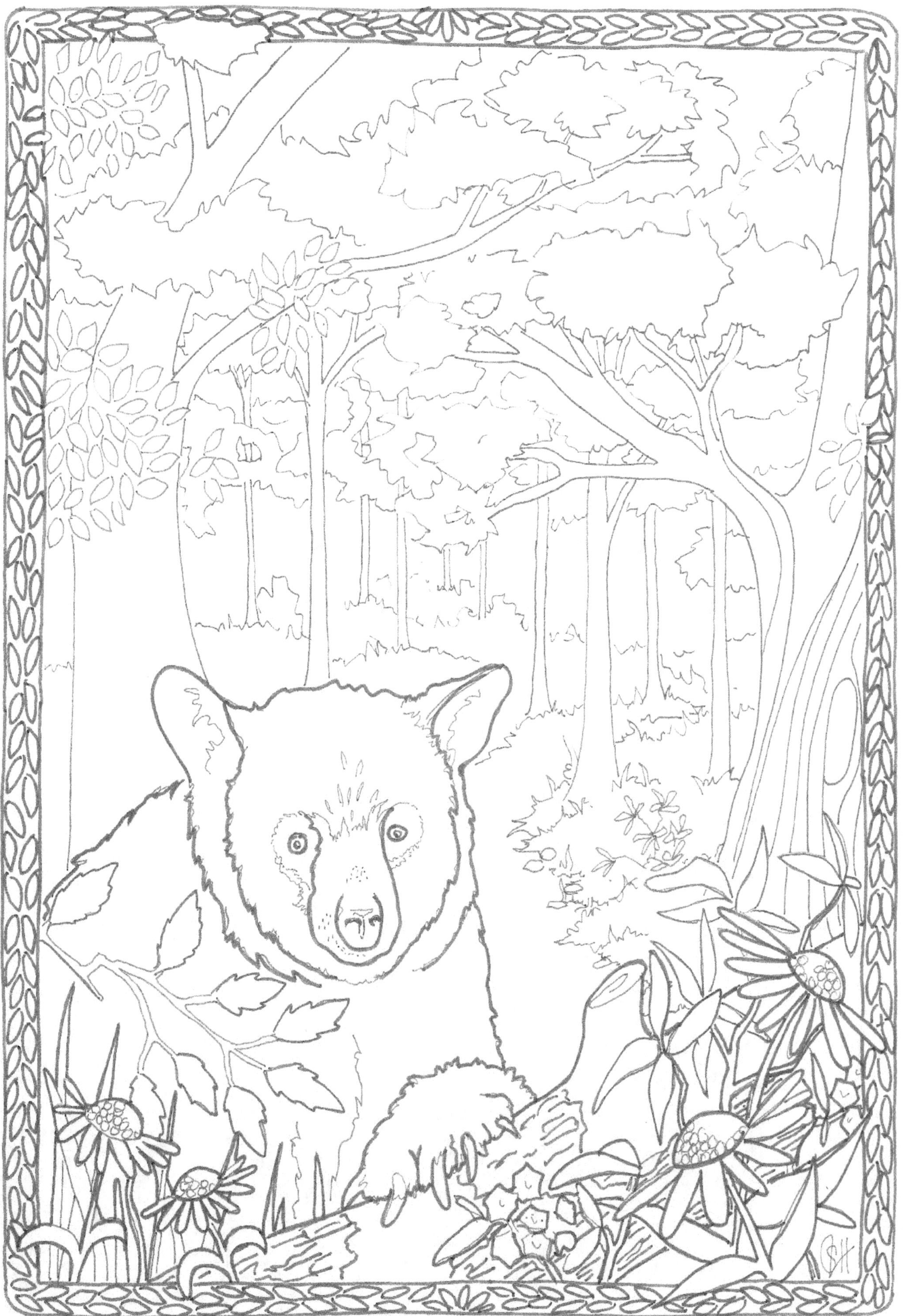

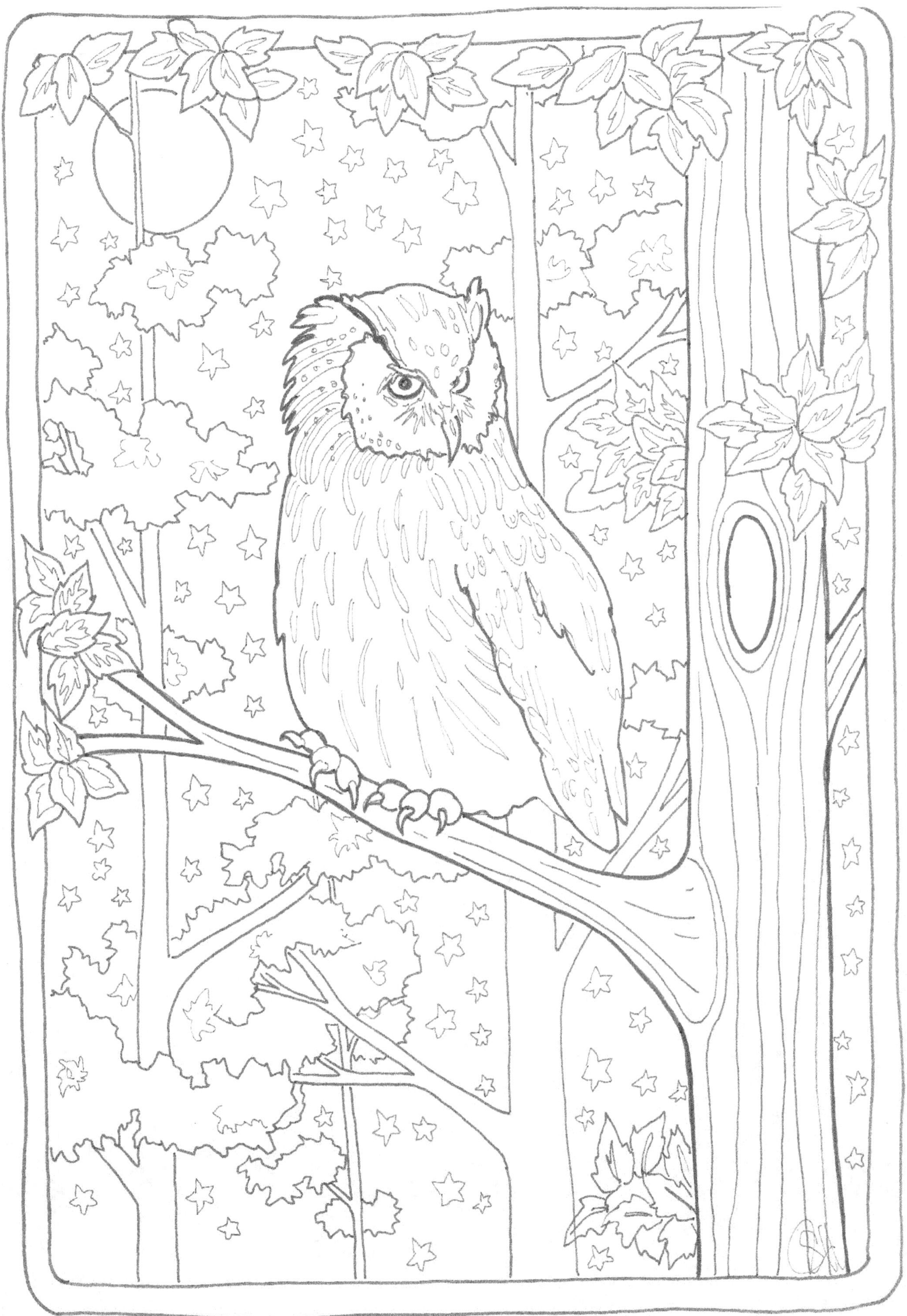

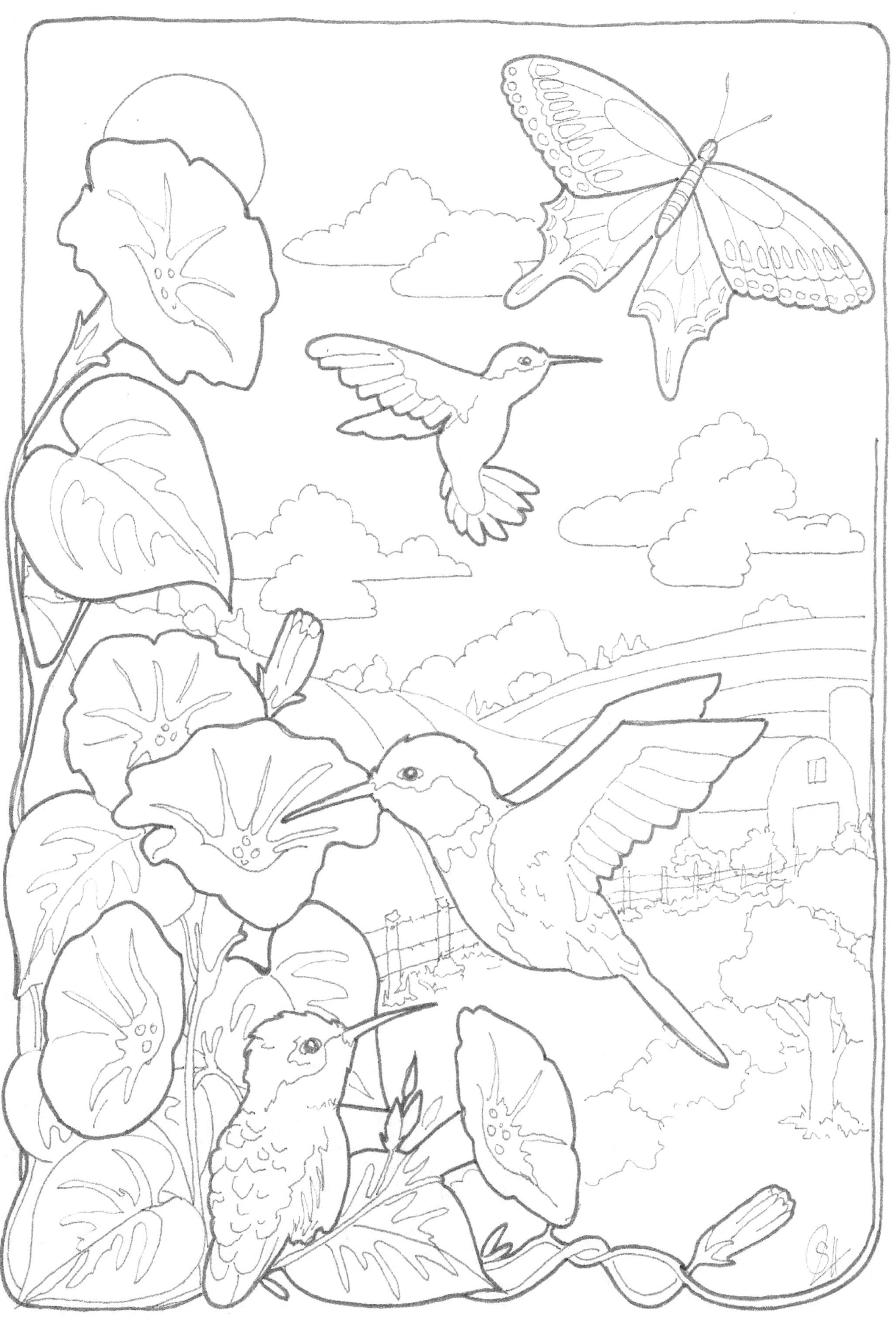

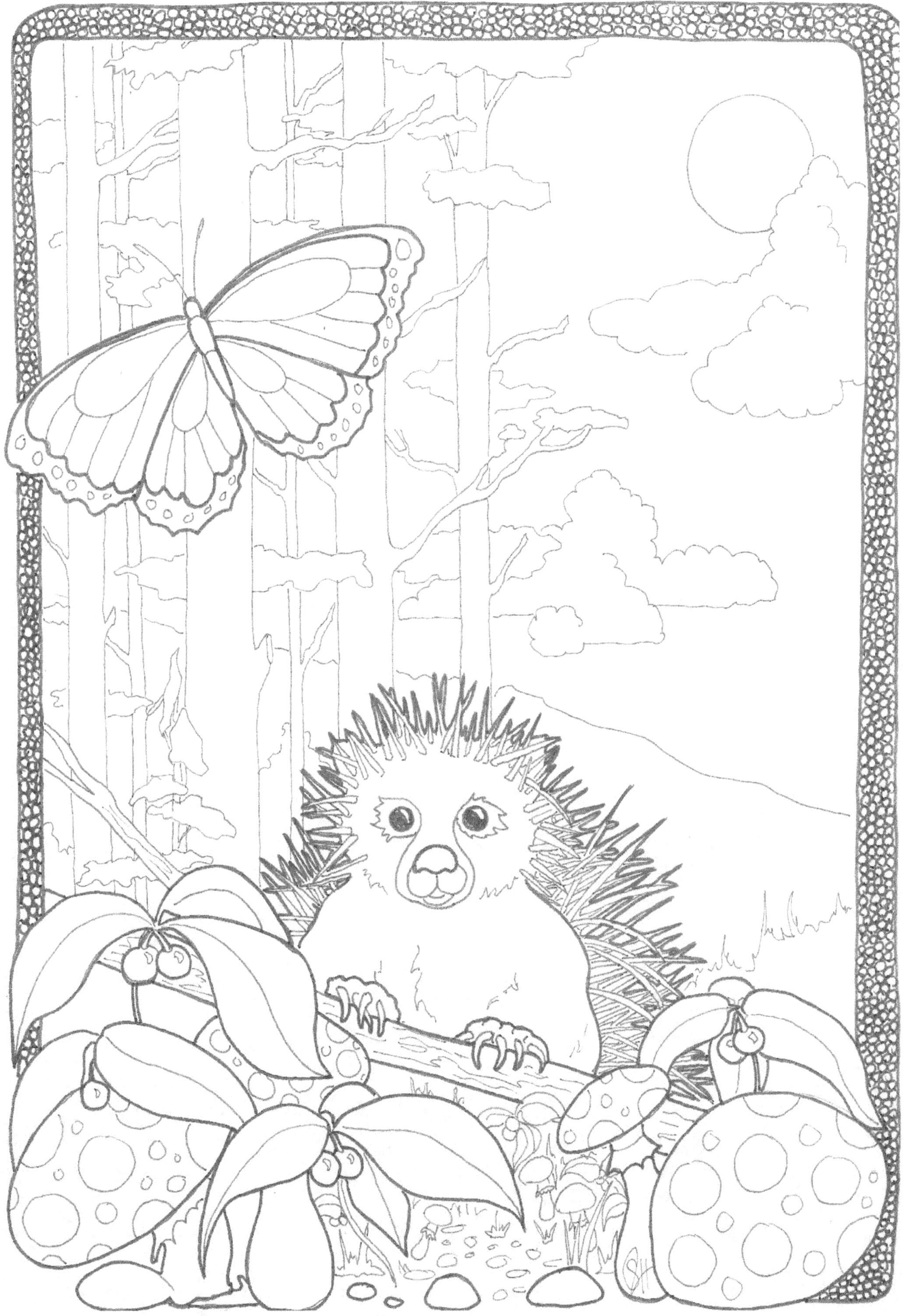

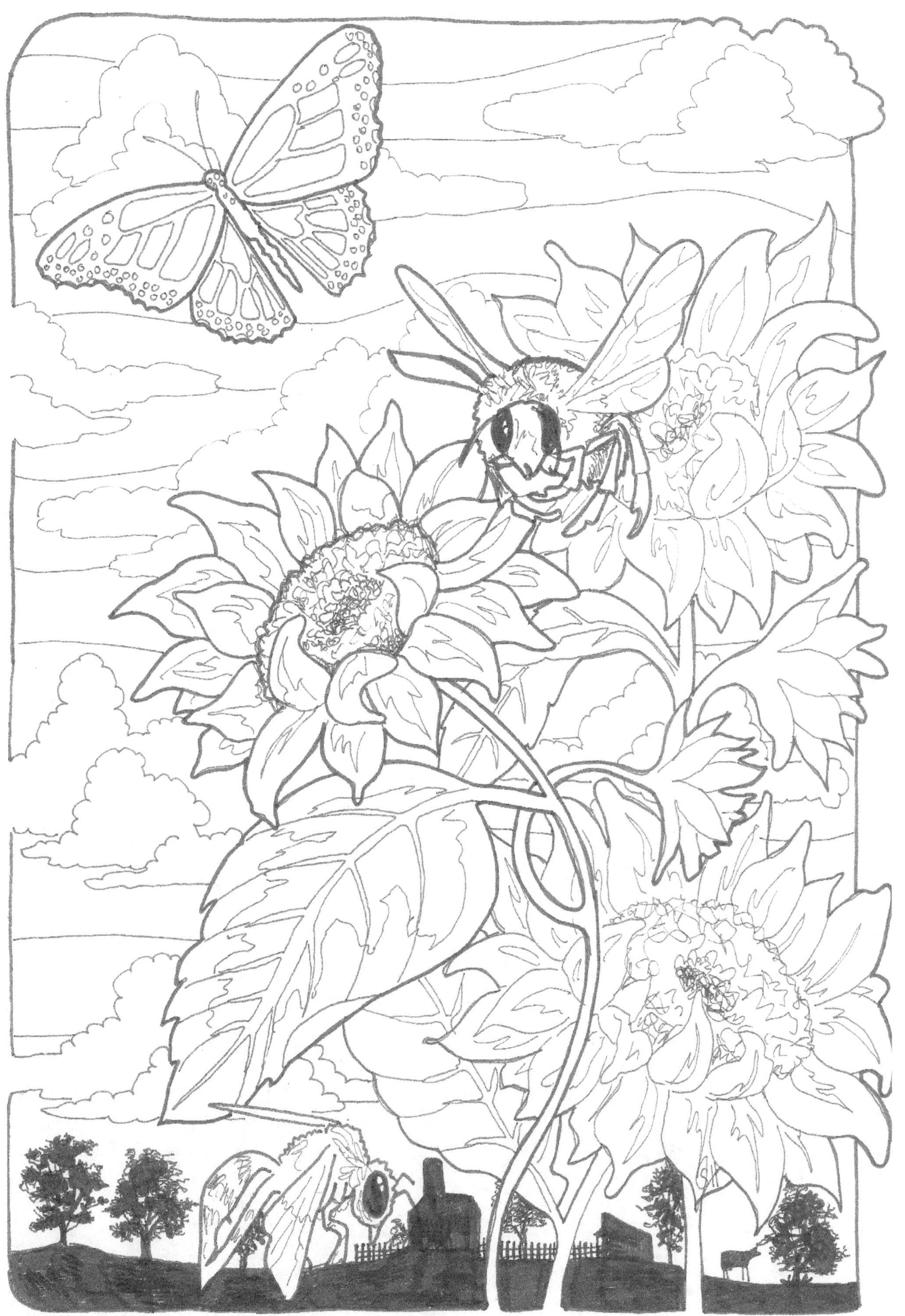

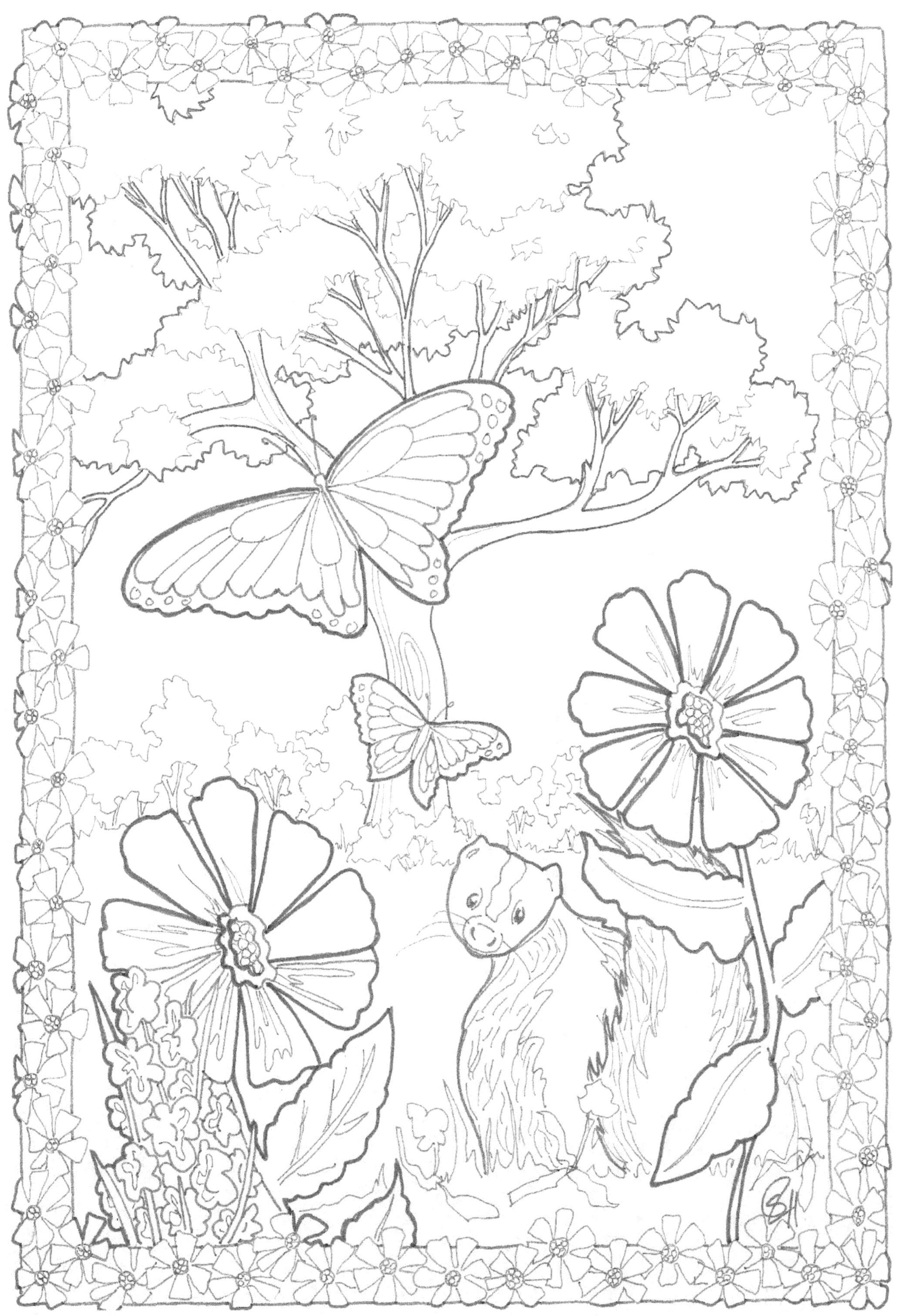

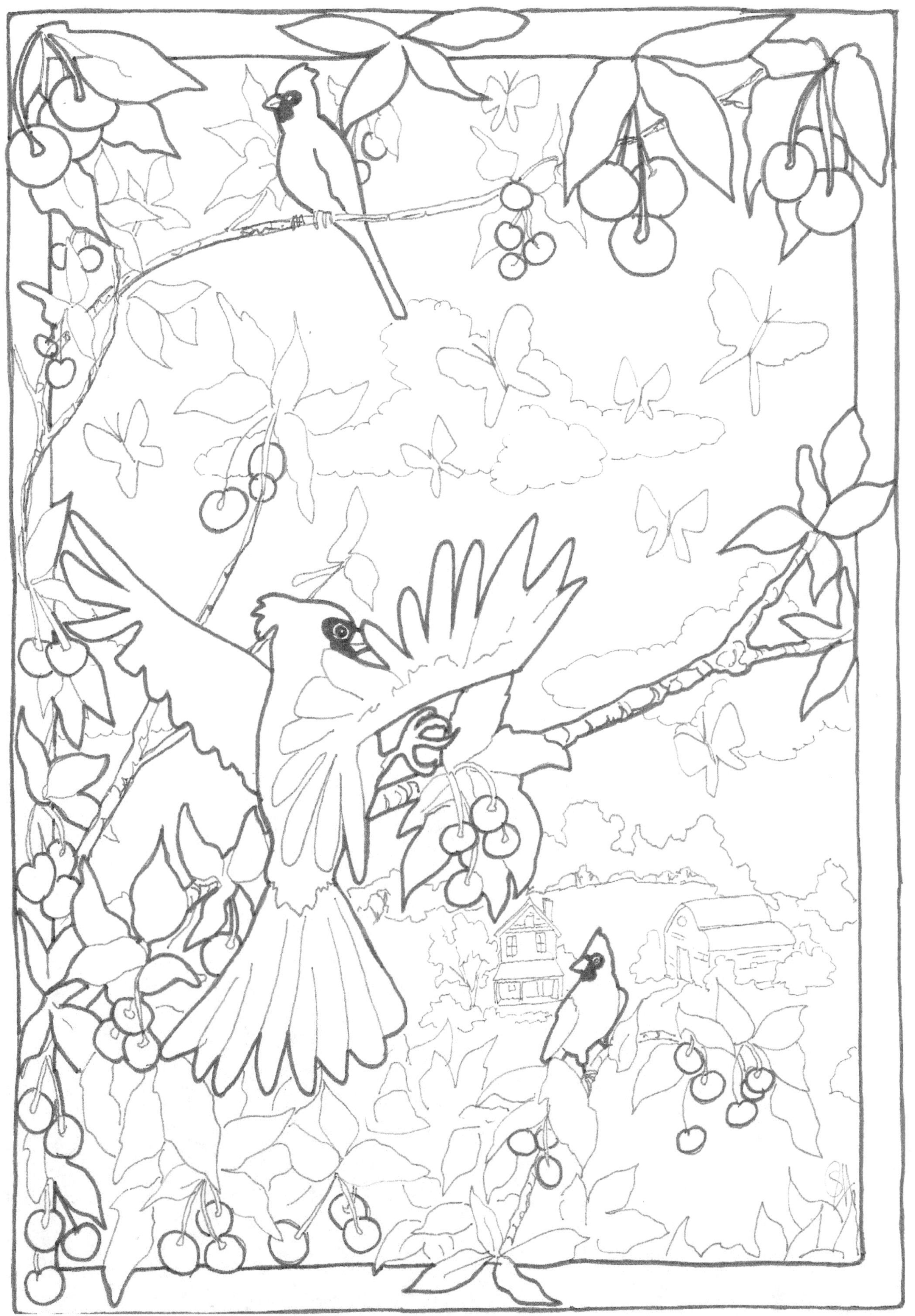

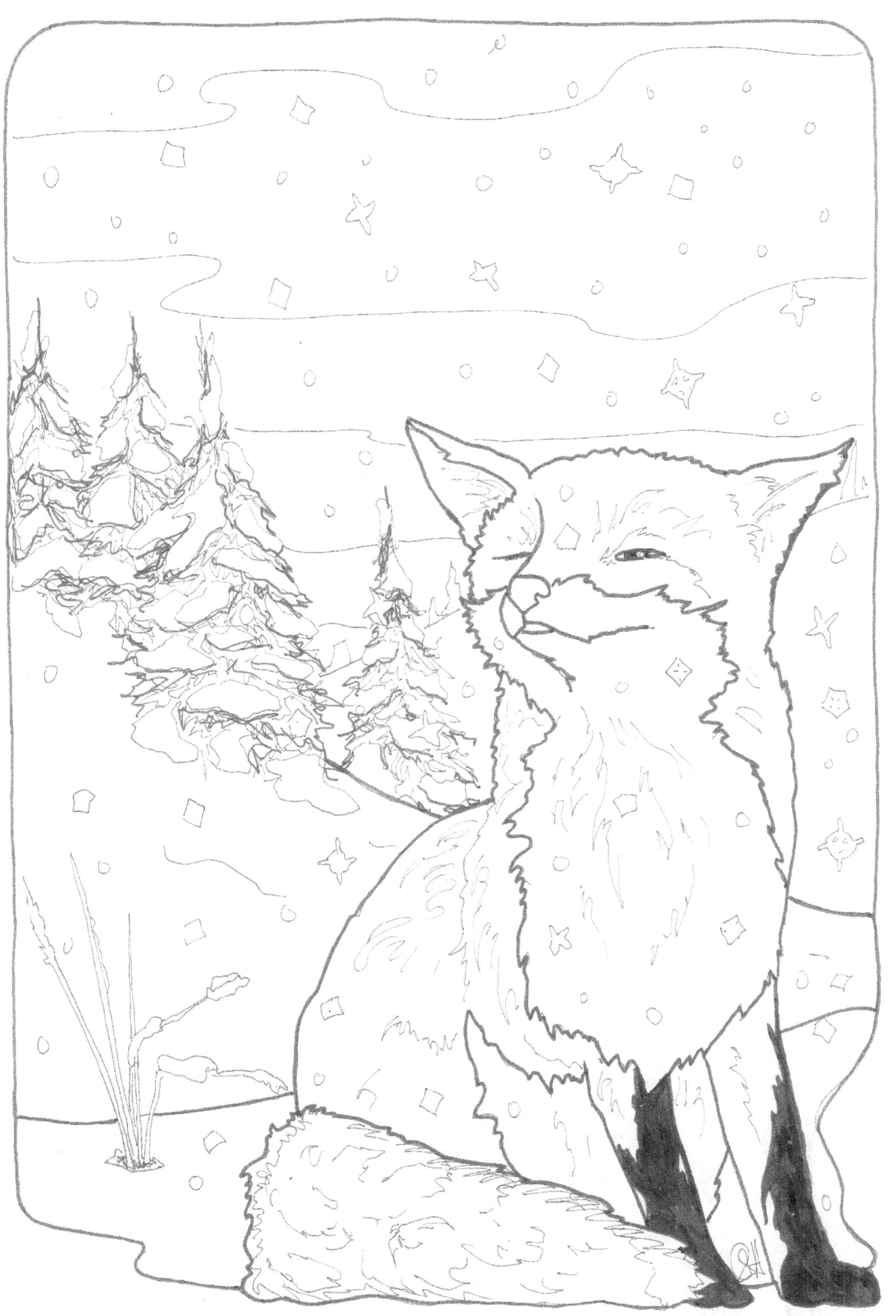

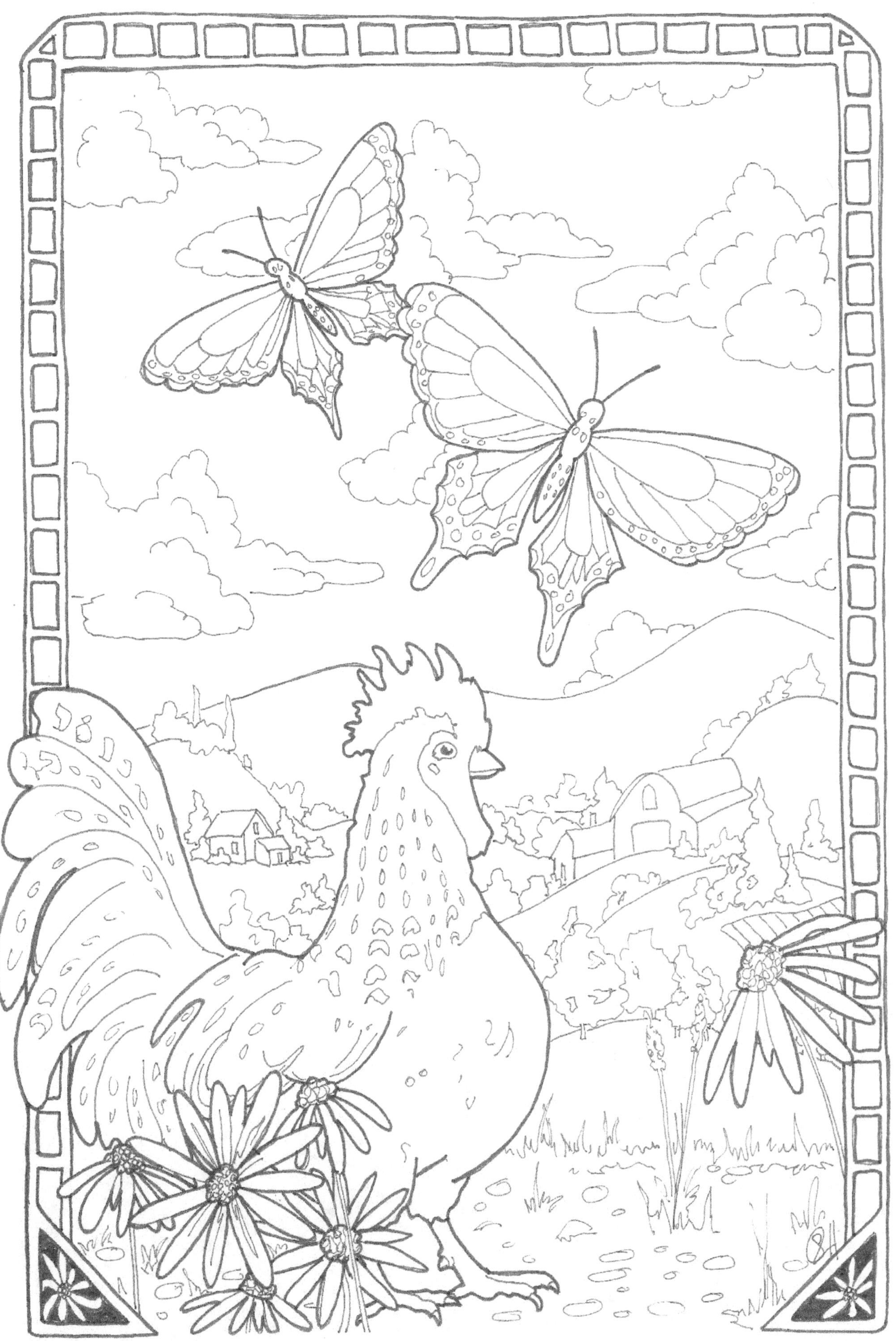

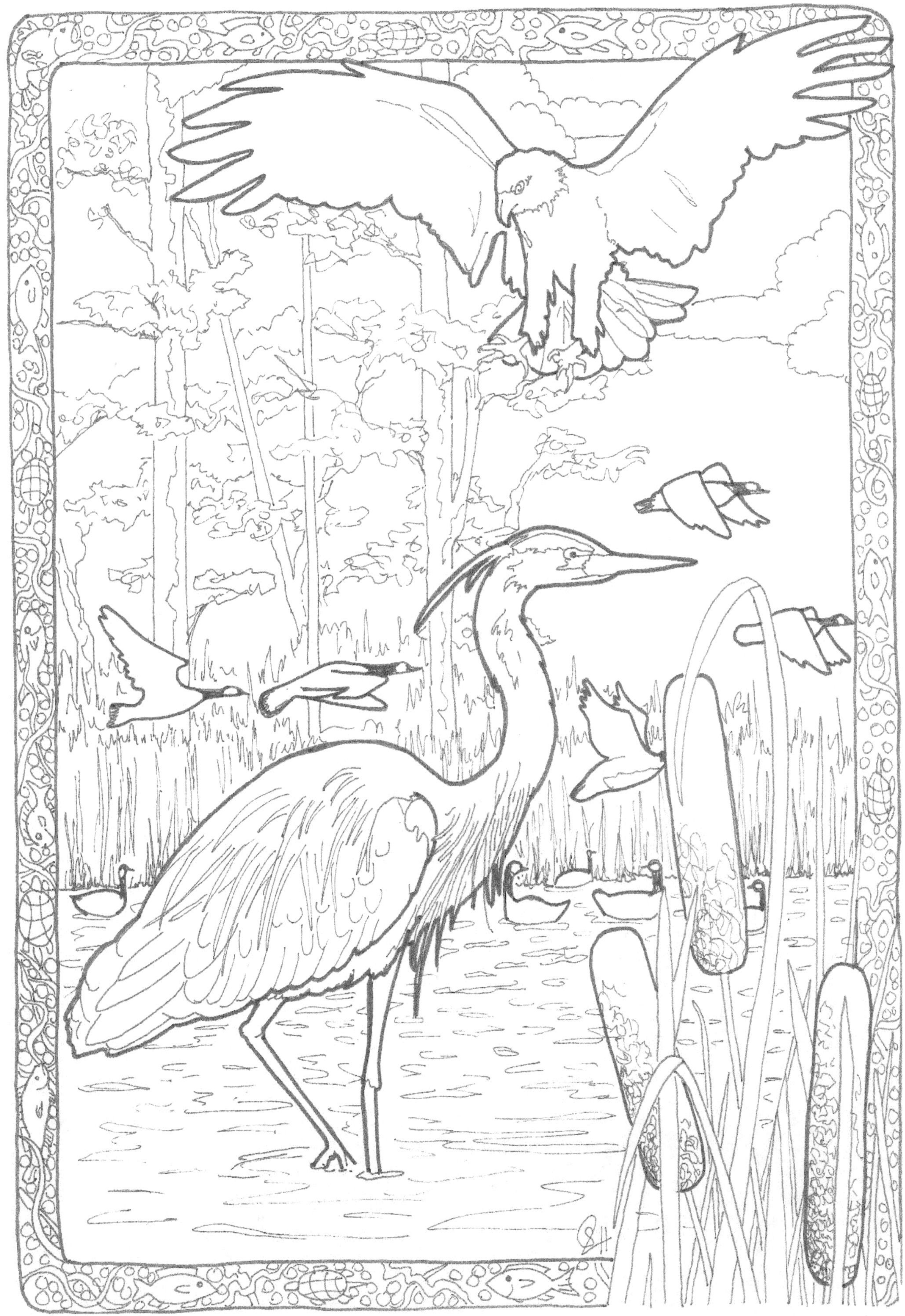

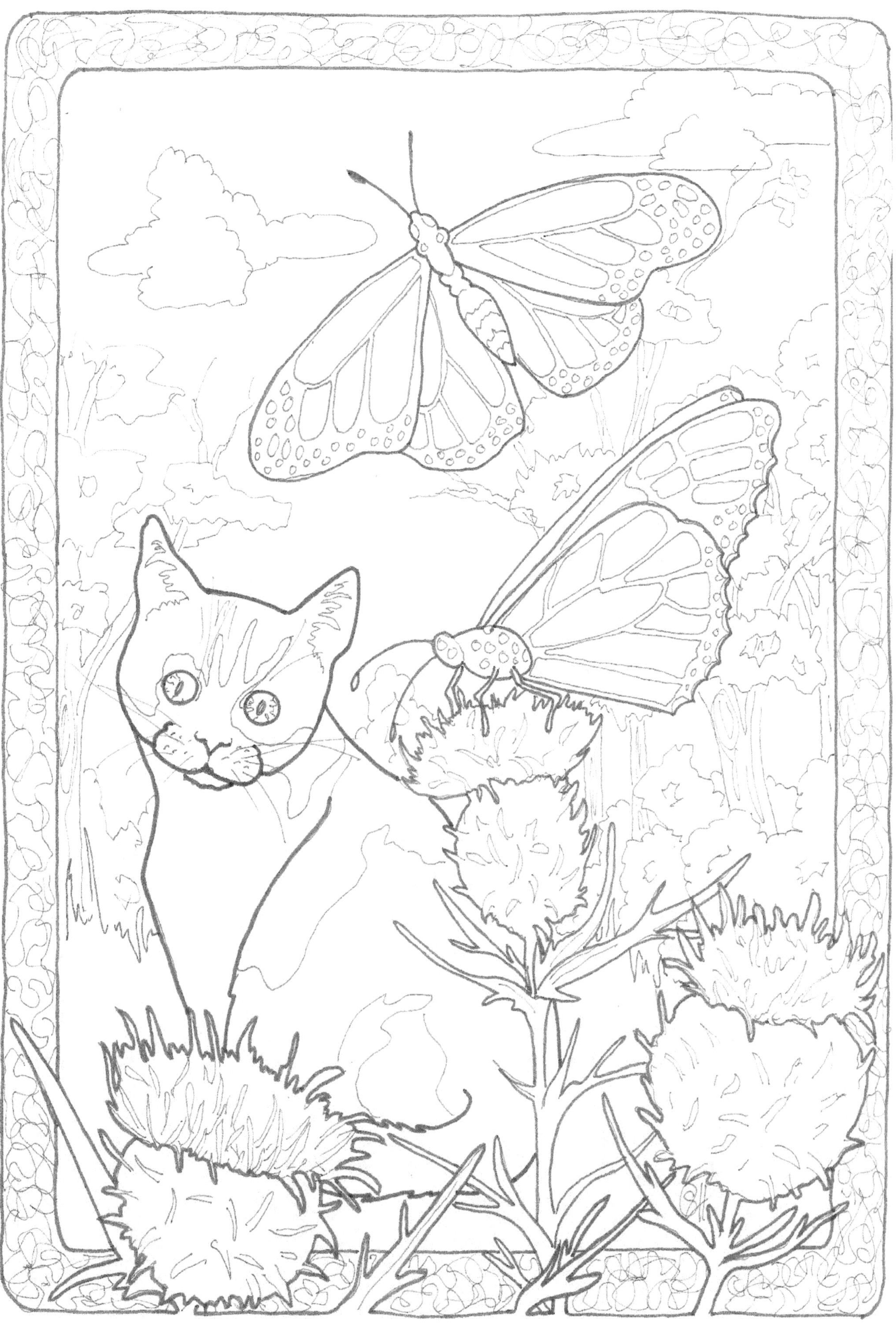

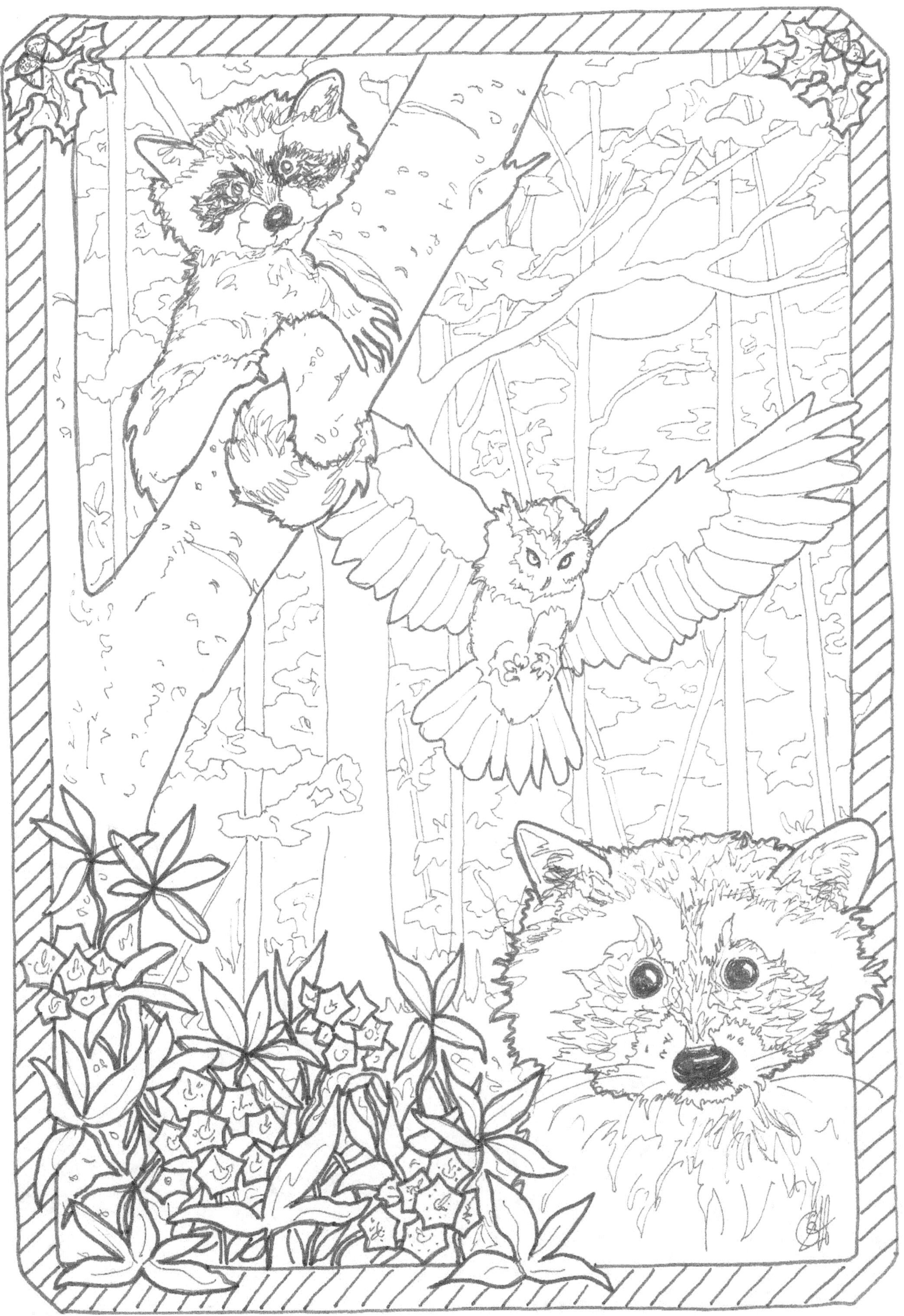

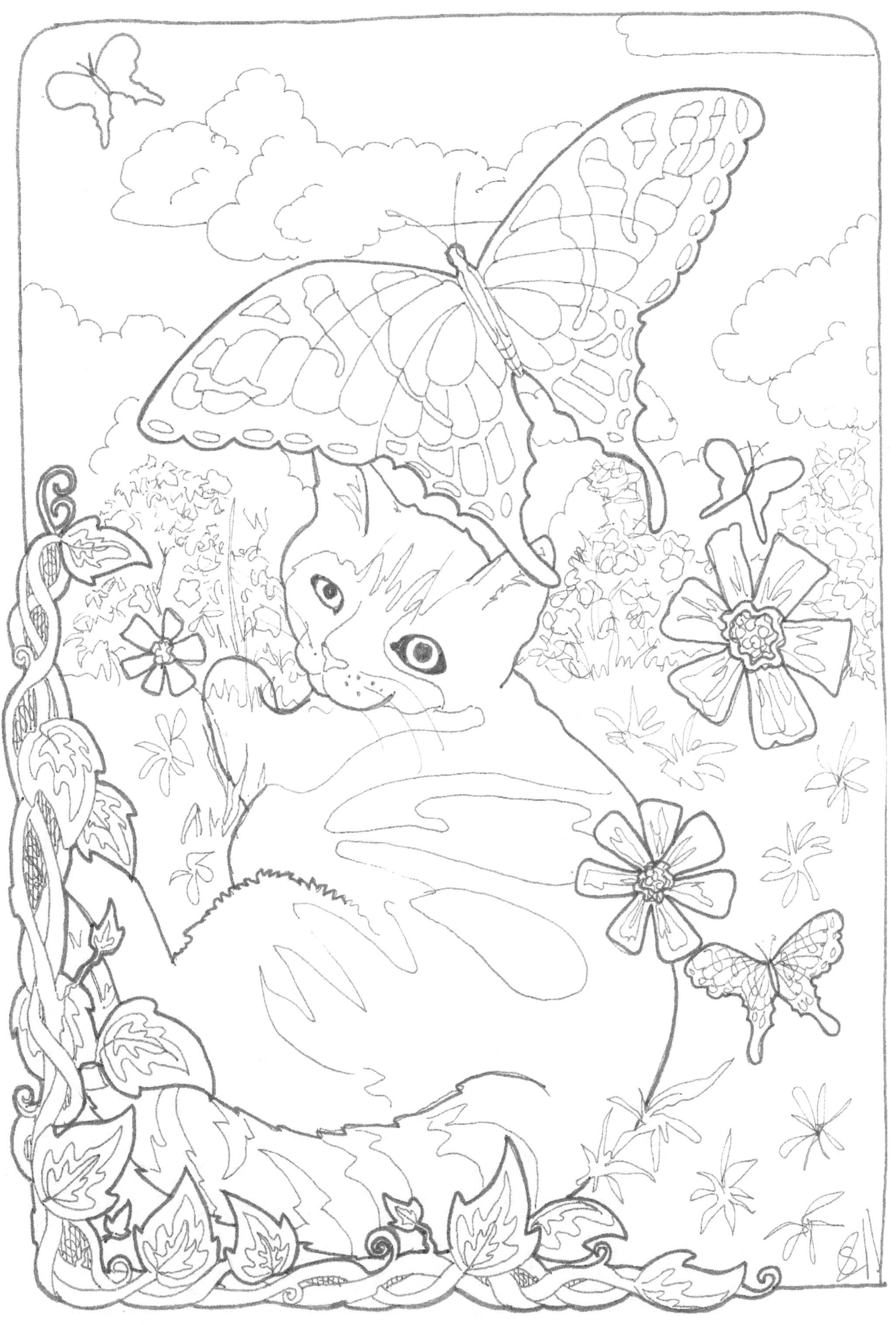

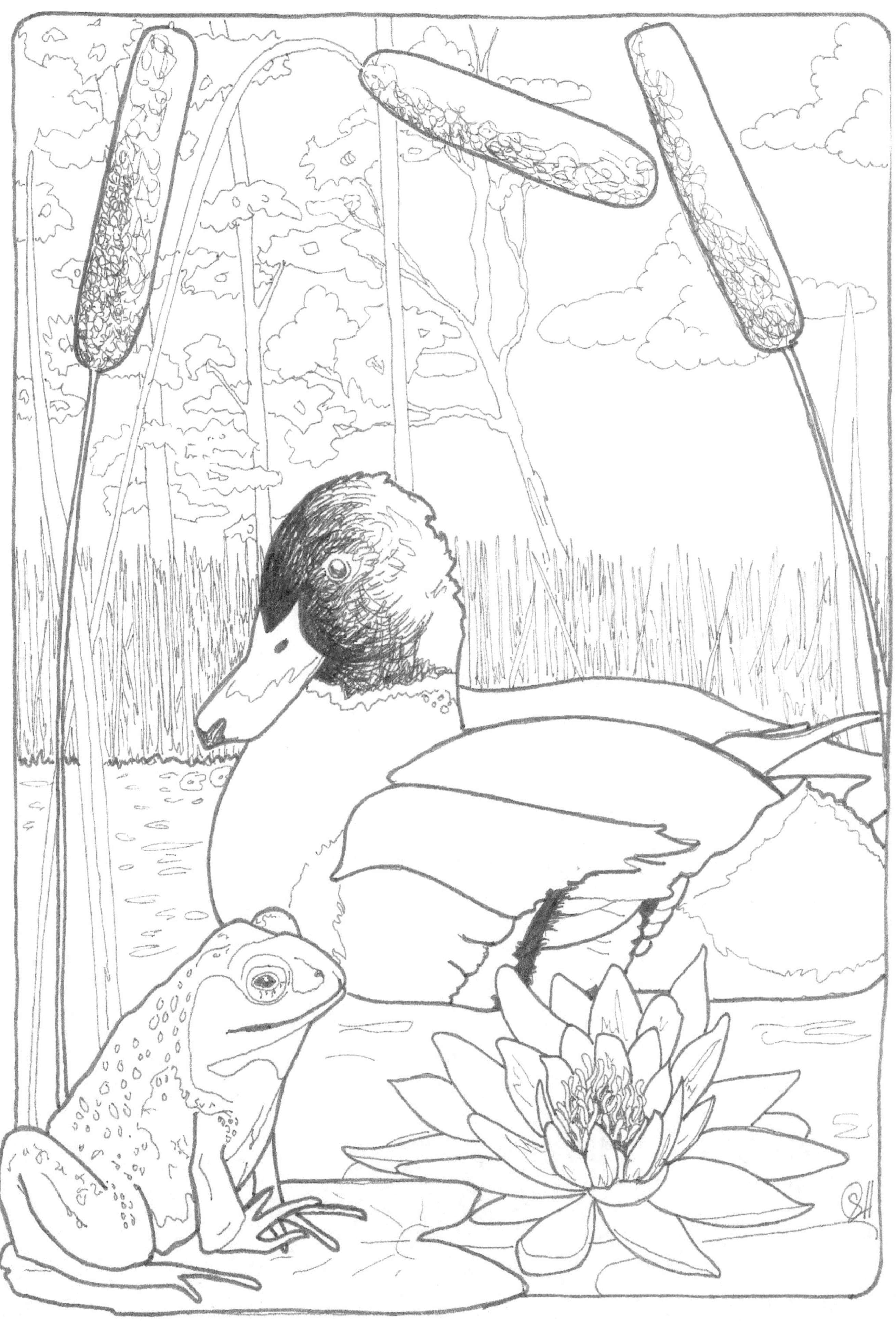

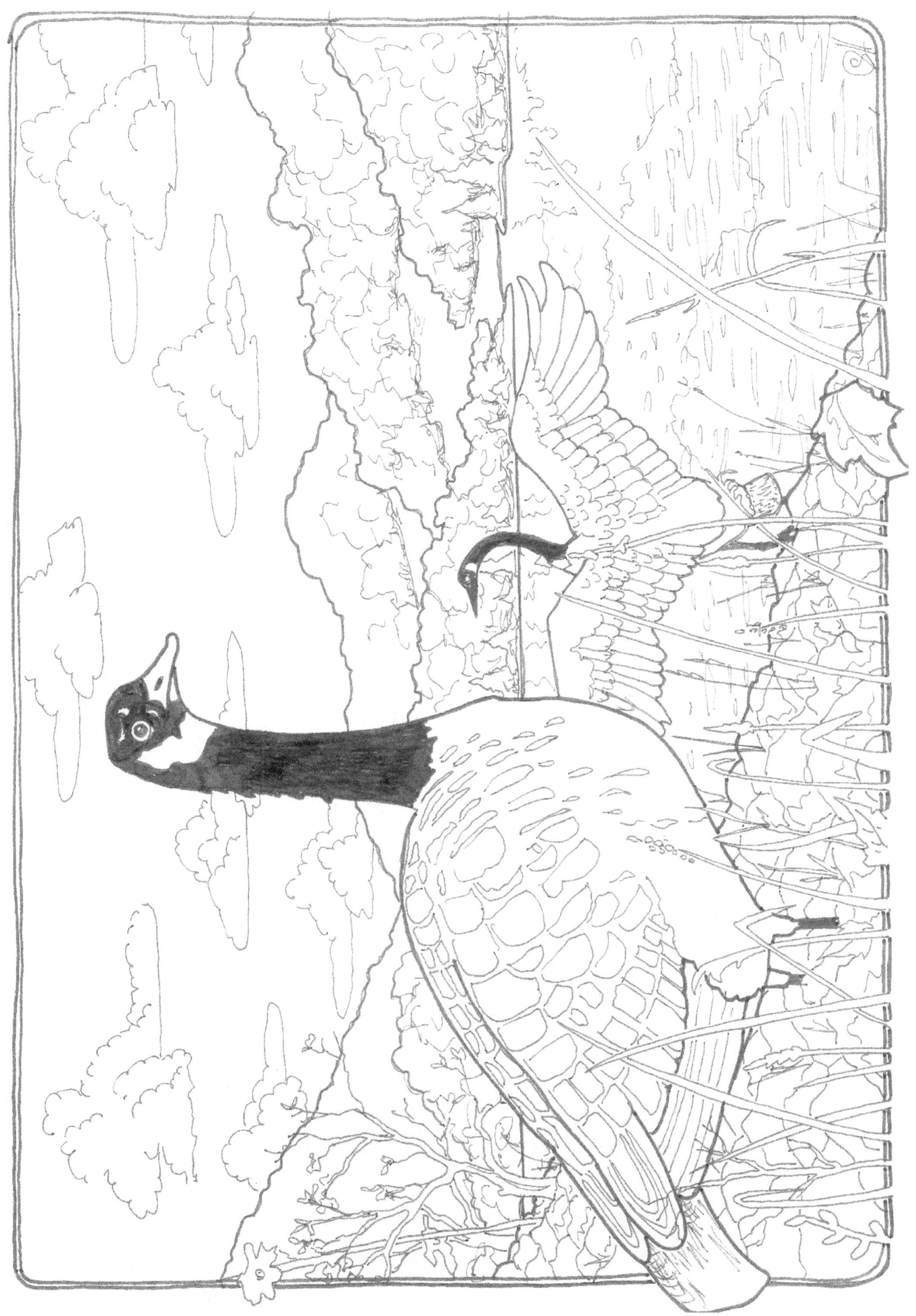